MILITARY SHIPS
DESTROYERS

BY JOHN HAMILTON

VISIT US AT
WWW.ABDOPUBLISHING.COM

Published by ABDO Publishing Company, PO Box 398166, Minneapolis, MN 55439.
Copyright ©2013 by Abdo Consulting Group, Inc. International copyrights reserved in all
countries. No part of this book may be reproduced in any form without written permission
from the publisher. A&D Xtreme™ is a trademark and logo of ABDO Publishing Company.

Printed in the United States of America, North Mankato, Minnesota.
042012
092012

Editor: Sue Hamilton
Graphic Design: Sue Hamilton
Cover Design: John Hamilton
Cover Photo: United States Navy
Interior Photos: All photos United States Navy except United States Naval Historical
Center-pgs 10, 11, & 29 (Admiral Zumwalt portrait).

ABDO Booklinks
Web sites about Military Ships are featured on our Book Links pages. These links are
routinely monitored and updated to provide the most current information available.
Web site: www.abdopublishing.com

Library of Congress Cataloging-in-Publication Data

Hamilton, John, 1959-
  Destroyers / John Hamilton.
     p. cm. -- (Military ships)
  Includes index.
  Audience: Ages 8-15.
  ISBN 978-1-61783-522-3
  1. Destroyers (Warships)--United States--Juvenile literature. I. Title.
  V825.3.H36 2013
  623.825'40973--dc23
                    2012005063

TABLE OF CONTENTS

DESTROYERS

United States Navy surface warfare ships come in three sizes. They include large cruisers. They also include small, economical frigates. In the middle are destroyers. They are not big, but they are very powerful.

XTREME FACT

New weapons and technology have made modern destroyers as deadly as many larger ships in the Navy's fleet.

The USS Stout sails on a mission in the Mediterranean Sea.

ARLEIGH BURKE-CLASS DESTROYERS

The newest type of U.S. Navy destroyers are Arleigh Burke-class destroyers.

The USS *Arleigh Burke* first sailed in 1991. Since then, more than 60 ships of this class have entered service. They replaced older Spruance-class destroyers.

The USS Arleigh Burke *sailing through rough seas in 1993.*

XTREME FACT

These ships are often called guided-missile destroyers. Instead of large guns, they use missiles as their main weapon.

MISSIONS

The main mission of destroyers is to protect other Navy ships, especially aircraft carriers. But modern destroyers can carry out many other kinds of missions. They can strike the enemy on shore, or far inland. They can shoot down enemy missiles and aircraft. They can attack other ships. They can even hunt and destroy enemy submarines.

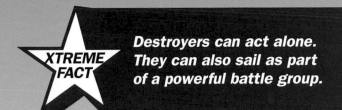

Destroyers can act alone. They can also sail as part of a powerful battle group.

The guided-missile destroyer USS Preble *training with the aircraft carrier* USS Ronald Reagan.

HISTORY

In the late 1800s, small boats armed with torpedoes became a threat to larger warships. These fast "torpedo boats" could dodge enemy fire. In response, the Navy built "torpedo boat destroyers" to protect its fleet. They were fast and maneuverable, and armed with large guns. They were especially useful during World War I and World War II. After World War II, large deck guns were eventually replaced with guided missiles.

The torpedo boat USS Porter *running sea trials in 1897.*

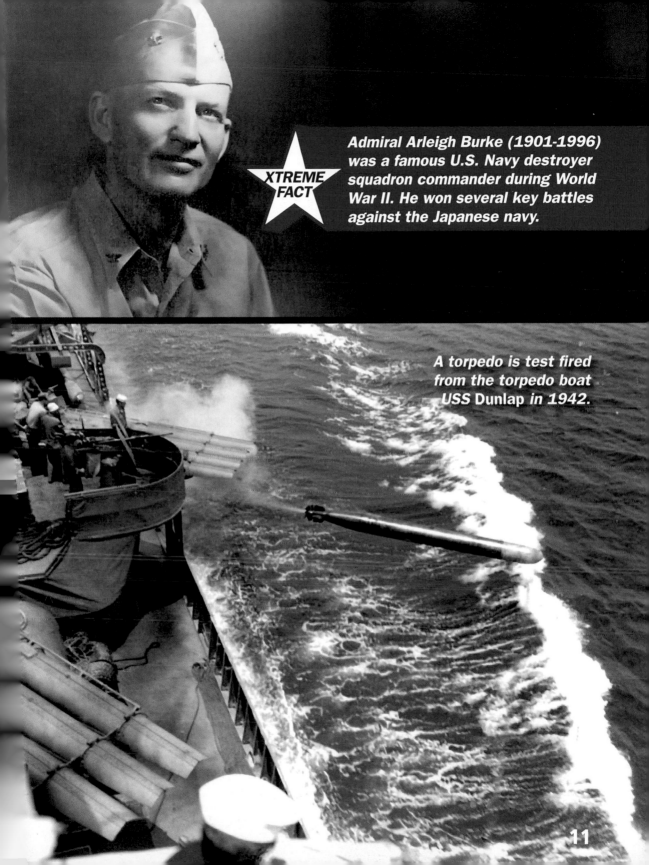

Admiral Arleigh Burke (1901-1996) was a famous U.S. Navy destroyer squadron commander during World War II. He won several key battles against the Japanese navy.

A torpedo is test fired from the torpedo boat USS Dunlap in 1942.

DESTROYERS FAST FACTS

Arleigh Burke-Class Specifications

Length:	**509 feet (155 m)**
Width (beam):	**66 feet (20 m)**
Displacement (loaded):	**10,636 tons (9,649 metric tons)**
Propulsion:	**Four gas turbine engines** **Two propeller shafts**
Speed:	**30-plus knots (35 mph/56 kph)**
Crew:	**32 — Officers** **348 — Enlisted**

The guided-missile destroyer USS Hopper *sails on a mission in the Pacific Ocean.*

ENGINES

Arleigh Burke-class destroyers are powered by four LM2500 GE marine gas turbine engines. They provide a total of 100,000 horsepower (74,570 kw) to two propeller shafts. This gives the ships a maximum speed of more than 30 knots (35 mph/56 kph).

A Navy technician checks one of the four LM2500 gas turbine engines aboard the destroyer USS Russell.

XTREME FACT

The same class of engine used in Arleigh Burke-class destroyers is also used in commercial airplanes, such as Boeing 767s.

AEGIS COMBAT SYSTEM

Arleigh Burke-class destroyers use the Aegis combat system. It relies on advanced radar and computers that track enemy ships, aircraft, and submarines. The Aegis system also guides missiles to enemy targets.

XTREME FACT

Aegis (pronounced ee-jis) is named after the shield of the Greek god Zeus.

The Aegis system uses powerful radar. The AN/SPY-1 radar is mounted on the hull. It detects enemy threats all around the ship. It can find air targets more than 288 miles (463 km) away. The Aegis system tracks more than 250 targets at the same time.

The Aegis combat system is used to launch a flight test of an SM-3 (Standard Missile Three) aboard the Navy destroyer USS Decatur.

SM-2 MISSILES

Arleigh Burke-class destroyers can fire dozens of SM-2 Standard Missiles. These guided missiles can intercept enemy aircraft and missiles up to 104 miles (167 km) away. They can be launched in bad weather if necessary. A destroyer's Aegis radar system helps guide the missiles to enemy targets.

An SM-2 Standard Missile launching from the USS Fitzgerald.

Destroyers fire missiles using the Mark 41 Vertical Launch System (VLS). It is hidden underneath the main deck.

An SM-2 launching from the Vertical Launch System aboard the USS O'Kane.

PHALANX CIWS

If an enemy aircraft or missile gets too close, the Phalanx CIWS (Close-In Weapon System) springs to life. It is a rapid-fire gun that automatically tracks targets. Its range is about 2.2 miles (3.5 km). Its Vulcan Gatling gun can shoot 75 tungsten armor-piercing rounds per second.

A Phalanx CIWS fires exercise rounds aboard the guided-missile destroyer USS Bulkeley.

The Phalanx system uses its own radar system to automatically track and destroy enemy air targets.

TOMAHAWK CRUISE MISSILES

Destroyers can fire TASM BGM-109 Tomahawk cruise missiles at enemy ships. They have a range of about 288 miles (463 km). They receive targeting information from satellites.

The USS Barry *launches a Tomahawk cruise missile.*

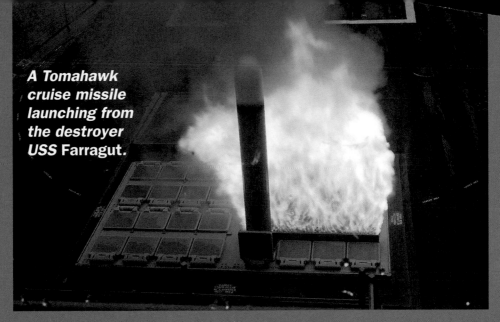

A Tomahawk cruise missile launching from the destroyer USS Farragut.

Destroyers can also attack far-away land targets. They use TLAM BGM-109 Tomahawk missiles for such missions. These missiles use radar to compare ground features with computer maps of the target. They can travel about 1,000 miles (1,609 km) to deliver their powerful explosive payloads.

XTREME FACT

Tomahawk cruise missiles travel at low altitude, which makes them difficult to detect and shoot down.

MK 45 GUN

Arleigh Burke-class destroyers are armed with an Mk 45 5-inch (12.7 cm) gun on the bow of the main deck. The Mk 45's main job is to defend against enemy ships. It can also attack aircraft or land targets. The Mk 45 can hit the enemy up to 13 miles (21 km) away.

Sailors load the Mk 45 gun aboard the USS Stockdale.

XTREME FACT

The most recent version of the Mk 45 gun is operated by a crew of three. They load and operate the gun below the main deck.

The Mk 45 gun is fired during a training exercise aboard the USS Pinckney.

ANTI-SUBMARINE WARFARE

Arleigh Burke-class destroyers use two kinds of sonar to detect hidden submarines. One sonar is located in the ship's bow. The ship also trails a sonar array on a long tether. It can drop down to the ocean's depths. When an enemy sub is detected, the destroyer can fire Mk 46 torpedoes to destroy the threat.

Sonar technicians monitor the Surface Anti-Submarine Combat System aboard the USS Momsen.

LAMPS Mk III Seahawk helicopters extend a destroyer's submarine detection. Seahawks can drop sonar buoys. When a sub is detected, Seahawks can fire torpedoes.

A Seahawk helicopter drops a recoverable exercise torpedo.

A Seahawk helicopter assigned to an anti-submarine squadron launches from the destroyer USS James E. Williams.

XTREME FACT

The most recent version of Arleigh Burke-class destroyers have a hanger in the stern that can permanently house two Seahawk helicopters.

THE FUTURE

The next generation of U.S. Navy destroyers will likely be Zumwalt-class warships. These futuristic-looking destroyers are designed to carry out many missions. They can bombard enemy land targets. They also protect Navy ships by shooting down missiles and aircraft. Their stealthy shape makes them hard for enemy radar to detect.

XTREME FACT

Admiral Elmo R. Zumwalt commanded Navy forces during the Vietnam War. He also served as Chief of Naval Operations until 1974.

A painting of the U.S. Navy's new DDG 1000 Zumwalt-class destroyer. The USS Zumwalt is scheduled for delivery in 2014.

GLOSSARY

DISPLACEMENT

Displacement is a way of measuring a ship's mass, or size. It equals the weight of the water a ship displaces, or occupies, while floating. Think of a bathtub filled to the rim with water. A toy boat placed in the tub would cause water to spill over the sides. The weight of that water equals the weight of the boat.

ENLISTED

A military service person who joined the armed forces, but is not an officer.

HULL

The hull is the main body of a ship, including the bottom, sides, and deck.

RADAR

A way to detect objects, such as aircraft or ships, using electromagnetic (radio) waves. Radar waves are sent out by large dishes, or antennas, and then strike an object. The radar dish then detects the reflected wave, which can tell operators how big an object is, how fast it is moving, its altitude, and its direction.

SEA TRIAL

The first test cruise of a newly constructed ship. It is the last step in construction.

Also called a "shakedown cruise," this first trip at sea may last from a few hours to several days. The ship's speed, maneuverability, equipment, and safety features are tested.

SONAR

Technology that allows ships and submarines to detect objects underwater by measuring sound waves. An "active sonar" system sends out a burst of sound, a "ping" that travels through the water. When the sound wave hits an object, such as a ship or underwater obstacle, the wave is reflected back. By measuring the reflected wave, sonar operators can determine the object's size, distance, and heading. "Passive sonar" detects the natural vibrations of objects in water. It is most often used by submarines, because sending out an active sonar signal might give away the submarine's position.

TOMAHAWK CRUISE MISSILE

A missile that can be launched from a ship, as well as from aircraft or submerged submarines. It has stubby wings, and can be used over medium- to long-range distances.

WORLD WAR I

A war that was fought in Europe from 1914 to 1918, involving countries around the world. The United States entered the war in April 1917.

WORLD WAR II

A conflict across the world, lasting from 1939-1945. The United States entered the war in December 1941.

INDEX